The Buddha of Silicon Valley

Mindfulness in Tech Startups

Table of Contents

Chapter 1. Introduction

Immerse yourself in our exciting Special Report titled "The Buddha of Silicon Valley: Mindfulness in Tech Startups." Venture with us into tech companies' heartland, where amidst the hum of innovation and churn of code, a serene transformation is underway. Discover how mindfulness is being woven into the fabric of startups, enhancing productivity and fostering a sustainable work culture. Witness the fascinating convergence of ancient wisdom and cutting-edge technology, birthing an ecosystem of calm within the continuous storm of technological advancement. Enthralling, insightful, and certainly a must-read, this report invites you to explore what is quickly becoming Silicon Valley's secret ingredient to success. This unique incorporation of mindfulness is truly setting a new precedent in the tech world. Act fast and get your copy today!

Chapter 2. The Dawning of Mindful Innovation

In the valley, amidst the neon blinks and constant hum of servers, a peculiar transformation is slowly unfolding. This metamorphosis, more of a cognitive shift than anything, is subtly disrupting conventional business models and paradigms. Entrepreneurs, investors, and even veteran tech gurus are embracing a surprisingly simple, yet deeply potent tool—mindfulness.

Mindfulness, in essence, is a state of being fully present, aware of where we are and what we're doing, and not overly reactive or overwhelmed by what's going on around us. In the relentless quest for success and growth, mindfulness is becoming the epicenter of personal and professional development, proving itself to be more than just a buzzword in the ever-evolving tech world.

2.1. The Mindful Revolution

The arrival of mindfulness within the walls of Silicon Valley is perhaps best interpreted as a harmonious convergence of ancient wisdom and modern technology. Emerging from monastic contemplative traditions, and passed down through centuries as a fundamental aspect of Buddhist philosophy, mindfulness has found its place in the heart of the tech industry.

This merger is not surprising. At its core, Buddhism emphasizes alleviating suffering by grasping the nature of reality. Taking a page from this wisdom, Silicon Valley has begun to approach problems differently. Adopting mindfulness not only humanizes technology, but injects a deeper sense of purpose and understanding into the psyche of business operations.

Companies are coming to recognize that while technological

superiority is crucial, the mental and emotional well-being of their workforce can no longer be neglected—the bottom line is impacted by both. As a result, an empathetic, focused, and healthy work culture is slowly becoming not just a feel-good bonus, but an imperative to survive the cut-throat competition.

This revolution has just begun. The tech world is starting to introduce mindfulness as a core aspect of their work culture and innovation strategy. As an example, Twitter and Google are not only investing in mindfulness workshops for their employees but are also creating dedicated spaces within their campus for mindfulness practices.

2.2. Mindfulness as a Strategic Advantage

The integration of mindfulness into business strategies has also started to reflect positively on the financial performance and creativity of tech startups. Businesses that encourage mindfulness are finding improvements in productivity, employee satisfaction, and ultimately corporate profitability.

Google's 'Search Inside Yourself' program—an innovative mix of mindfulness, neuroscience, and emotional intelligence—is one example of strategic mindfulness application. Employees are taught effective mindfulness and meditation techniques designed to enhance focus, reduce stress, and promote creative thinking.

Research has indicated that mindfulness training can dramatically improve attention and flexibility, qualities necessary for thriving in a fast-paced, innovative environment. By adopting these strategies, companies are not only nurturing more focused, stress-resilient employees but are also aiding the development of strategic, big-picture thinkers.

Mindfulness also fosters enhanced emotional intelligence among team members. The practice encourages empathy, helping to build bridges between individuals with varying perspectives, meeting the crucial need for a more inclusive, diverse, and harmonious work culture in the tech industry.

2.3. Mindfulness and Ethics in Tech

In addition to improving productivity and profitability, mindfulness plays a substantial role in the realm of ethics in technology. In recent years, some tech giants have come under scrutiny for questionable business practices, unethical use of data, and for creating products that perpetuate harmful behaviors such as excessive screen time and digital addiction.

Mindfulness practices encourage individuals to pause and reflect on the implications of their actions—prompting consideration of consequences that expands beyond quarterly profitability reports.

Integrating mindfulness into standard operating procedures allows companies to navigate the complex intersections of technology, society, and ethics with a greater degree of thoughtfulness. It inspires developers and executives alike to question and reflect on the potential societal impact of their work, creating technological innovation that is not just advanced or creative, but responsible and ethical.

As a result, companies that genuinely practice mindfulness may find themselves less likely to fall into ethical missteps, saving them from regulatory penalties and reputational damage.

2.4. Looking Ahead: A Mindful Future

As mindfulness practice continues to thrive in the technological incubator that is Silicon Valley, the ripple effects are projected to be far-reaching. While it's often associated with the individual, mindfulness carries transformative potential for organizations, whole industries, and even broader societal structures.

As tech startups continue to form the bedrock of innovative solutions and advancements, the intentional and strategic inclusion of mindfulness in their operations could quite likely redefine success parameters in the tech industry.

From managing stress and promoting creativity to driving ethical decision making and fostering a sense of shared purpose among employees, mindfulness might just be the missing piece of the puzzle Silicon Valley has been looking for. As this consciousness grows, we can only expect to see more harmonious, sustainable, and ethical innovation flourishing amidst the silicon chips and server racks. With mindfulness, a new dawn is indeed breaking over the landscape of technological innovation.

In the ultimate analysis, the success of integrating mindfulness will lie within the acceptance of its powerful simplicity. Silicon Valley's spontaneous drive and propensity for a forward-leading vision might well prove an ideal breeding ground for this confluence of ancient wisdom and modern innovation. While the journey is just beginning, the mindful innovation that is slowly dawning in Silicon Valley promises an extraordinary evolution, the echoes of which will reverberate throughout the tech world and beyond.

Chapter 3. Unraveling the Mind-Machine Connection

The mind-machine connection is a vast concept that expands beyond the realms of the common understanding. This connection is becoming an integral factor in the tech revolution stirred up by Silicon Valley startups. They are investigating, researching, and implementing mindfulness techniques to enhance human cognition and elevate human-computer interaction.

Silicon Valley's leading tech advocates believe that fostering this balance between the human mind and technology ushers in a more sustainable work culture. They claim that the seeds of tech innovation are planted in the fertile soil of human intellect, which thrives on calmness and mindfulness.

3.1. Pioneering a New Equilibrium

In a world where technology is sometimes seen as disruptive or distracting, it may seem counterintuitive that Silicon Valley, the symbolic vortex of this tech-storm, has turned towards age-old wisdom to find equilibrium. Today's Silicon Valley startups are creating an authentic dialogue between the digital frontier and the ancient practice of mindfulness, leading to the birth of the mind-machine connection.

The pioneering tech firms are cultivating mindfulness, by diving into the digital wave and harnessing it for mental well-being. They carve one-on-one sessions, workshops, and group meditations right into their weekly work routines. Using tech tools, applications, and software, these trendsetters are building an ecosystem of meditation and thoughtfulness within their corporate structures, ushering in an era of collaboration between human minds and machines.

3.2. Data Emphasizing Mindfulness

Seeing the mind and body as interconnected, tech startups have begun using data to drive mindfulness. Wearable technology provides biofeedback, illustrating one's physiological response to stress and giving insight into their mindfulness states. By coupling this understanding with advanced AI algorithms, they've created internal apps that monitor these physiological markers, suggesting moments for reflection or mindfulness.

Furthermore, Silicon Valley startups are encouraging data-driven meditation. Advanced machine learning techniques are being utilized to classify and predict meditation states, offering real-time insights that help individuals deepen their mindfulness practices. This approach moves traditional meditation techniques into the realm of quantifiable science, offering metrics that provide actionable advice.

3.3. Creating Mindful Products

Silicon Valley's innovative startups are not only integrating mindfulness into their work culture but also weaving this concept into their product design. They are crafting technological solutions that not only resolve issues but also foster calm, promote ease of use, and offer peace in an otherwise hectic world. These products are designed with a deep understanding of the human mind, building a bridge between technological functionality and mindfulness, encouraging a more harmonious interaction between individuals and their digital tools.

3.4. Mindful Coding: A New Approach

Coding, the very nucleus of any tech startup, is also being

transformed by this mindfulness wave. A mindful approach to coding emphasizes attentive, focused, and stress-free development. Silicon Valley's coding gurus are highlighting 'coding flow', where coders submerge themselves completely into the task at hand, fostering innovation and reducing coding mistakes. Studies have showcased that a calm and focused mind can improve productivity, ensure cleaner code, and reduce bugs, leading to time and cost efficiencies.

3.5. Mindfulness: A Boost to Innovation

Perhaps the most exciting aspect of this mind-machine connection is its potential to enhance the power of innovation. Mindfulness allows entrepreneurs and technologists to tap into a pivot of creativity that isn't accessible in a stressed mindset. Silicon Valley is creating spaces where silence and reflection are valued, and where ideas can germinate from a place of calm focus. Mindful meetings and technology-detox zones are becoming commonplace, facilitating a culture of thoughtfulness and promoting out-of-the-box thinking.

The mind-machine connection in Silicon Valley startups is more than an interplay of technology and neuroscience; it's shaping up to be a significant catalyst for not just human-computer interaction, but for human-human collaboration as well. The convergence of Eastern wisdom and Western technological prowess is ultimately enabling a more mindful, productive, and sustainable work culture in the world's tech capital.

In conclusion, unraveling the mind-machine connection is not merely a mental exercise but a profound exploration into how ancient wisdom can enhance our interaction with modern technology. In the auspicious hands of Silicon Valley's brightest, this exploration is instigating shifts that might alter the way we perceive and make use of technology. As they say: watch this space.

Chapter 4. Silicon Valley: The Unexpected Sanctuary

From the outside, Silicon Valley presents a picture of a bustling hub of innovation, where technological dreams are born and come to fruition. Start-ups hustle, engineers dream-inspire-code, and venture capitalists scheme up the next big thing. This maeligan of ambition and aspiration, however, conceals an unexpected sanctuary, a quiet revolution, that's shaping not only the way people work but also their consciousness.

4.1. The Genesis: Mindfulness in the Valley

The concept of mindfulness, an age-old practice rooted in ancient Buddhist philosophy, promotes focused awareness on the present moment, drawing upon inner wisdom to transcend the incessant churning of thoughts. Once an esoteric practice restricted to the realms of spirituality and wellness, it's now finding growing traction in the heart of technological innovation - Silicon Valley.

Tech entrepreneurs, developers, venture capitalists, and everyone in between are embracing mindfulness as a potent tool. It's a way to alleviate rising stresses and anxieties associated with intense work environments, encouraging a paradigm shift from mind-full to mindful. This transition is giving rise to a new strain of thought, leading to the creation of an ecosystem fostering tranquillity amidst the tick-tock of a relentless technological marathon.

4.2. Tech Titans Pave the Way

The mindfulness revolution within Silicon Valley isn't a testament to a collective awakening of tech-giants alone. It's rather an acknowledgment that turning inwards can lead to outer success. A notable proponent of this school of thought is Twitter and Square co-founder, Jack Dorsey, who attributes his resilience and clarity to a hardcore mindfulness regime involving meditation retreats and silent affirmations.

Industry leader Google offers 'Search Inside Yourself' programs, encouraging employees to incorporate mindfulness into their routines. The results? Enhanced creativity, heightened focus, and improved leadership skills. As more organizations join the mindfulness bandwagon, it's imperative to delve deep and discern the driving forces behind it.

4.3. Detangling the Stress Web: The Mindful Antidote

Start-ups are risky. Launching a product into an already saturated market, meeting investor expectations, and dealing with frugality until you hit stability all add to the everyday stress. Mindfulness is turning out to be a balm for this overworked, overstimulated, and stress-stricken tech community. The practice is helping them switch gears, inducing relaxation responses, and fostering a culture of calm that is critical to the innovation process.

A study conducted by the American Psychological Association showed that mindfulness can dampen the activity in the amygdala and boost connections in the prefrontal cortex, areas of the brain linked with stress and anxiety response. This underscores mindfulness as a cost-effective and potent antidote to stress-related issues prevalent within the tech landscape.

4.4. Mindful Action: Enhanced Productivity

Beyond the obvious benefits of reducing stress, the principles of mindfulness are proving to be tools for enhanced productivity. By encouraging mental agility, mindfulness allows for greater flexibility in cognitive processes. It steers the brain into 'focused-mode', a state of deep work, boosting creativity, improving problem-solving abilities, and catalyzing innovative ideas. Mindfulness is allowing techies to shift gears from a tangential whirl of distractions to a more steady, centered outlook.

4.5. Mindfulness as a Cultural Catalyst

As more and more Silicon Valley companies embrace mindfulness, it is not only transforming the individuals but also the workplace culture. It's fostering a culture of empathy, understanding, and mutual respect, a sharp contrast to the infamous 'brogrammer' culture that has been heavily criticized for its lack of sensitivity.

Mindfulness nudges tech companies to recognize workers' needs beyond the physical - the need for balance, for mental peace, and emotional well-being. It encourages a non-judgmental workspace, where people feel heard and are treated with compassion. The leadership, too, is evolving, with managers developing a mindful leadership approach, leading with empathy rather than authority.

4.6. Reinventing the Wheel: From Burnout to Balance

In essence, mindfulness is causing an uplifting disruption in Silicon Valley. It's no silver bullet, neither a panacea for all workplace woes, but it certainly offers the tools to navigate the stormy waters of the tech world. Silicon Valley, in embracing mindfulness, is reinventing its entrepreneurial culture, resetting its drive from reckless burnout to sustainable balance. The spirit of fearlessness remains, but with the added humility of acknowledging vulnerabilities.

The technological haven of Silicon Valley can aptly be lauded as the unconventional garden where the seeds of mindfulness are not only being sown but nurtured with care. The mindfulness wave is reshaping the landscape of this epicenter of innovation - where the Buddha of the East silently communes with the technology gurus of the West.

As mindfulness makes its way deeper into the realms of technology, one thing is certain. This ancient wisdom won't merely remain an anecdote of the past, but a guiding light for a more aware, compassionate, and productive technology industry of the future.

Chapter 5. Navigating Stress: Redefining Startup Culture

Silicon Valley's characteristic energy isn't all creativity and inspiration; it often summons a deep-seated stress that permeates through the ranks of a startup. The race to innovate, secure funding, and bring products to market at lightning speed can foster an intensely stressful environment. Whereas tech startups once stumbled towards burnout on their quest for market domination, today the industry is waking up to the notion of sustainable productivity.

This dramatic cultural shift is being driven by an unexpected ally: The centuries-old practice of mindfulness.

5.1. Towards Sustainable Productivity

Research suggests that a stressed employee is an unproductive one. According to studies conducted by the American Psychological Association, stress can lead to decreased focus, impaired memory, hindered decision-making capabilities, and generally reduced cognitive functioning. This isn't news for any startup leader who's witnessed the toll of long work hours and relentless pressure on their team.

Yet, in the heart of the tech world, a profound realization is reshaping the working culture: Sustainable productivity requires an actively managed stress level. Enter mindfulness, an ancient practice emphasizing presence, awareness, and acceptance. In its simplest form, mindfulness is about staying in touch with the present moment, viewing life experiences objectively and devoid of judgement.

Mindfulness allows us to recognize stressors, giving us contentment and clarity of thought that provides a strong foundation for building sustainable productivity.

5.2. Mindfulness as Stress Management

Early adopter tech startups have begun instituting group meditation sessions, encouraging mindful breaks, and offering training on mindfulness techniques. These initiatives are not just about keeping employees happy—they move to redefine what it means to cultivate a successful workforce.

The first step to combat stress is to name it, a process simplified by regular mindfulness practice. By acknowledging stress and its triggers, employees can detach themselves from their sources, preserving their cognitive capacities for tasks at hand.

Apart from the individual benefits, group meditation sessions foster a sense of collective calm and camaraderie in the workspace. Employees who meditate together share an experience that can have powerful bonding effects, decreasing interpersonal tensions and propelling synergistic collaboration.

5.3. Promoting Focus and Creativity

Mindfulness is no one-trick pony; its effects go beyond stress management. A study conducted at the University of California demonstrated a direct correlation between mindfulness and increased focus. An enhanced ability to concentrate influences not just productivity but also creativity.

In an industry that relies heavily on novel ideas and ingenuity, creativity is a critical asset, and it thrives under conditions of undivided focus. Mindfulness, by promoting single-tasking over multi-tasking and the quality of work over quantity, can lead to a surge of groundbreaking ideas.

Today's enlightened startups are incorporating mindfulness into their daily routines, realizing the fundamental truth that their success hinges on more than the quality of their codebase or the efficacy of their sales pitches. It resides in the minds of their teams.

5.4. This is Just the Beginning

The mindfulness revolution within Silicon Valley is still in its infancy. Yet the early effects are already being felt, with notable increases in productivity, improved interpersonal dynamics, and more robust creativity cycles reported across the industry.

The journey to lower stress, better focus, and increased creativity has started with the adoption of mindfulness. This long-hailed Asian philosophy and practice has found fertile ground in the soil of startup culture and poised to harvest productivity gains in unimaginable ways.

This unforeseen symbiosis of ancient philosophy and modern technology may just hold the secret to the next wave of innovation and productivity in Silicon Valley. This is the dawn of a transformative era for tech startups, where they're redefining their culture, not by racing against time, but by taking the time to slow down and breathe.

Chapter 6. Productivity and Peace: The Tech Balancing Act

In the hustle and bustle of Silicon Valley, where creativity is cranked up to a frenzied speed and pressure percolates every corner, guiding measures like mindfulness seem to emerge as an unlikely companion. But, as we venture deeper, it becomes evident that the art of mindfulness isn't just a coping mechanism, it's an amplifier of productivity, a springboard to success.

6.1. The Yin and Yang of Startups

Startups foster innovation, creativity, and rapid evolution, making them exciting, albeit intense, ecosystems. This whirlwind of productivity is sustained by motivating employees to constantly push the envelope, catalyzing bursts of innovation. Yet this relentless drive can lead to burnout, staff turnover, and a significant drop in productivity. In this frenetic milieu, mindfulness provides the necessary calm, the yin in the startup yang, allowing individuals to find equilibrium in the chaos of creation.

Mindfulness, the Buddhist practice of observing one's thoughts and emotions non-judgmentally, fosters heightened focus, boosts emotional intelligence, and develops resilience — the optimal set of tools to nurture a balanced and sustainable tech venture. Startups have recognized this hidden treasure, and the ancient tradition is now being enthusiastically adopted by the young companies.

6.2. Mindful Programming: Coding in the Now

One domain where mindfulness has made a significant impact is programming. Coding is a taxing process that demands high levels of concentration, logical thinking, and creativity. It's easy for developers to get lost in the labyrinth of code, leading to exhaustion and decreased productivity. Mindfulness provides a map to navigate this maze, allowing programmers to remain centered in the present moment, subsequently improving code efficiency and quality.

Implementing practices such as mindful breaks, wherein programmers take short pauses to practice breath-focused mindfulness, can dramatically improve focus and reduce coding errors. Further, promoting a company culture that supports mindfulness can significantly decrease burnout, thereby enhancing overall team productivity.

6.3. The Mindful Meeting: A New Paradigm

Meetings are an essential part of any organization. However, their effectiveness is often questioned, especially in startups where too many ideas compete for limited time and resources. This is where the mindful meeting comes into play.

Mindful meetings reimagine standard business gatherings through the lens of present-centered awareness. Participants are encouraged to listen actively, respond rather than react, and engage in empathetic discussions. This eliminates unnecessary conflict, reduces the amount of meeting fatigue, and fosters collaborative problem-solving.

Structured activities, such as a few minutes of collective silence at the beginning and the end of the meeting, can create a mindful atmosphere. Techniques like the 'talking stick' method, wherein only the person holding the stick talks while others listen attentively, can promote active listening and ensure each voice is heard and respected.

6.4. Building Resilience: The Mindful Way

Startups are rife with challenges and uncertainties. Funding shortfalls, product adoption issues, employee turnover – the list of potential problems is long. Such tribulations can cause significant stress, affecting both the individual's and the organization's performance.

Mindfulness practices can serve as a buffer against these adversities, helping individuals cultivate resilience and maintain composure even in challenging scenarios. Techniques like mindfulness-based stress reduction (MBSR), which combine mindfulness meditation and yoga, can significantly strengthen emotional robustness, improve problem-solving skills, and boost team and individual productivity.

6.5. From Mindfulness to Mindful Leadership

Mindfulness isn't just beneficial at an individual level. When exhibited by leaders, it can trickle down to influence the entire organization. Mindful leaders are aware, authentic, and compassionate, embodying a leadership style that not only fosters enhanced productivity but also nurtures a culture of trust and transparency. They are observant and reflective, making them adept at identifying problems early and finding feasible solutions.

Moreover, mindful leaders radiate calm and positivity, essential in fast-paced startup environments where stress is often the order of the day. Their presence positively impacts the collective energy of the team, leading to a more engaged, motivated, and, inevitably, productive workforce.

The intriguing interplay between mindfulness and productivity highlights Silicon Valley's ongoing quest to blur the lines between the ancient and the modern, the spiritual and the scientific, the mindful and the materialistic. This crossover illuminates a new path, enabling the creation of an ecosystem that amalgamates peace and productivity. The outcome is a nurturing work environment that not only drives success but also ensures the well-being of its most crucial asset – its people.

Chapter 7. Mindfulness Methods: From Meditation Rooms to Apps

Over the years, mindfulness methods have evolved in the tech companies of Silicon Valley as they wrestle with the challenges of the fast-paced and high-stress environment. These unique approaches range from classic meditation rooms and training programs to innovative mindfulness apps and other digital tools. This tapestry of methods aims to improve workers' overall well-being, boost productivity, and foster a healthy work culture.

7.1. Cultivating Calm: Meditation Rooms in Silicon Valley

Traditionally, the quest for mindfulness begins with a special corner to practice meditation. Companies in Silicon Valley are increasingly dedicating spaces specifically for meditation. These 'quiet rooms' or 'humming rooms' are sanctuaries where employees can either meditate in solitude or even join group meditation sessions during lunch hours or after a grueling day.

To ensure full comfort and relaxation, teams of interior designers infuse these spaces with minimalistic aesthetics and natural elements. Low light, warm colors, acoustic installations, and comfortable seating make these rooms the ultimate escape. Images of rolling landscapes, serene oceans, or even the Milky Way provide visual cues that transport a fatigued mind to places of tranquillity.

Taking a closer look at these meditation rooms, one thing stands out: simplicity. The design is carefully stripped down to the bare minimum. The idea is to eliminate distractions and, therefore, help individuals concentrate. Often, employees can also find basic meditation necessities in these rooms - cushions, mats, or mindfulness bells.

Meditation rooms have become an integral part of the workplace landscape, as mindfulness advocates often emphasize the need for a physical space in the office for personal reflection, rest, and mental rejuvenation.

7.2. Mindfulness Training Programs

A parallel branch of mindfulness proliferation in the workplaces of Silicon Valley has been professional mindfulness training programs. For many fervent converts, mindfulness is more than a tool; it's a life skill that needs careful training under experts' guidance.

These programs vary in their rigor, length, and format. Some of these stretch for months, while others are compressed into a fast-paced two-week course. The most common forms are in-person lessons, where mindfulness coaches offer employees techniques for focused attention, stress reduction, and emotion management.

Silicon Valley's leading companies often bring in prominent mindfulness teachers for these courses. Employees learn different meditation techniques, mindful listening, and even mindfulness-based leadership skills in these sessions. Often these programs are blended with webinars, e-learning courses, and one-on-one virtual sessions, meeting the need for both proximity and flexibility.

One unique aspect of these training programs is the dynamic blend of mindfulness teachings with the practicalities of tech workplace challenges. Techniques are taught in a work-contextualized way, equipping employees with tools to handle stress, manage tech burnout, enhance productivity, and cultivate leadership skills.

7.3. Stay Mindful: The Rising Tide of Mindfulness Apps

Digitalization seeped its way into the sphere of mindfulness practice as well, birthing a new market segment: mindfulness apps. These digital tools are redefined to fit into the smartphone era and into the pockets of professionals seeking tranquillity amidst chaos.

Mindfulness apps pack convenience, usability, and a wide variety of features. These apps often provide a library of guided meditation sessions, calming music tracks, and soothing nature sounds. They may also include features like mood trackers, digital journals, and reminders—effectively creating a comprehensive mindfulness platform for their users.

Silicon Valley's startups themselves have made significant strides in developing mindfulness apps. Headspace, Calm, and Insight Timer are leading examples of mindful meditations and stress reduction tools that have been highly popular in the tech community.

These apps also leverage cutting-edge technologies like machine learning and data analytics to provide personalized meditation plans. Users receive recommendations based on their daily stress levels, issues they're dealing with, or specific mindfulness goals. This precision fitting of technological advancements into age-old mindfulness techniques signals a groundbreaking overlay of the ancient and the modern.

7.4. Virtual Reality: An Auspicious Union of Technology and Mindfulness

In the quest for more immersive mindfulness practices, virtual reality (VR) marks the latest frontier. Silicon Valley companies are exploring the potential of VR to provide deeply immersive meditation experiences.

Virtual reality headsets transport individuals into sublime landscapes or serene environments, such as a peaceful forest, a quiet beach at sunset, or beneath a sky filled with vibrant stars. Users can quickly escape stresses of the work environment and immerse themselves into calming scenarios that foster relaxation and meditative focus.

Companies like TRIPP, Inc. are working on VR meditation experiences that enable individuals to meditate in fantastical environments. Think of floating in the cosmos amidst a symphony of stars or meditating in an underwater coral garden surrounded by gracefully swimming sea creatures.

In essence, mindfulness in Silicon Valley's landscape has been a journey of fusion, a harmonious blend of age-old practices and digital innovation. It's about using available tools to arrive at a place of quiet, to manage the noise of the world outside and the tempest within. From classic meditation rooms and mindfulness classes to mindfulness apps and virtual reality experiences, mindfulness practices are being incorporated into every aspect of work life. This variety ensures that every individual, regardless of his or her preferences, has access to an effective mindfulness tool. Silicon Valley has thus reshaped the ancient art of mindfulness to meet the needs of the digital age, setting a new precedent for the tech world worldwide.

Chapter 8. The Impact on Creativity and Problem Solving

As much as Silicon Valley teems with relentless progress and unbridled innovation, it also thrums with a unique energy: the collected calm of mindfulness. This convergence of an ancient practice with state-of-the-art technology has unfurled a revolutionary change, notably in the realms of creativity and problem solving. This is a domain of keen interest, especially since these areas power the ceaseless engine of technological leap and disruptive advancements in the Valley.

8.1. The Age of Mindfulness and Creativity

The relationship between mindfulness and creativity is not new. Historical anecdotes and recent studies suggest that the practice of mindfulness often results in increased creative output. This needs further exploration, especially in the context of the tech industry buzzing with agile minds and relentless invention.

Mindfulness, by definition, is the deliberate act of focusing one's attention on the present moment, a practice encapsulated in the Buddhist tradition. It sounds paradoxical, as the tech industry is future-oriented, always working to develop the 'next big thing.' However, philosophically, mindfulness and creativity converge at one point: they both begin in the present.

Creativity rests on a delicate perch, one tossed in the whirlwind of stress, deadlines, and constant pressure regularly experienced in the tech world. Mindfulness, however, offers an antidote – it trains the mind to clear out unnecessary clutter and devote its resources to the task at hand, fostering an environment conducive to creative thinking. Regular mindfulness practices, such as meditation, have been proven to increase neuronal connections in brain areas associated with creative thinking.

8.2. Mindfulness Meets Problem Solving

When it comes to problem-solving, the prowess of mindfulness comes into glaring focus. There are several problem-solving methods tech companies implement, from structured logical frameworks to brainstorming or design thinking. However, when a problem is particularly gnarly or complex, it requires a novel approach, something that veers from the well-trodden path. This is precisely where mindfulness can add unparalleled value.

By fostering a state of calm alertness, mindfulness cultivates an environment apt for lateral thinking—a type of creative thinking that necessitates looking at problems from different perspectives, often resulting in unorthodox solutions. In a state of mindful presence, the mind can efficaciously switch between divergent thinking, generating many ideas, and convergent thinking, combining those ideas into the best result.

Taking a leaf from Google's 'Search Inside Yourself' program, other tech companies have started to appreciate the merits of mindfulness practices in problem-solving. Employees are encouraged to take a few minutes of 'mindful moments' to collect their thoughts before diving headfirst into problem-solving. These short moments bring about an awareness of the present moment, reducing anxiety over the problem and inducing a calmer state of mind.

8.3. Case Studies: Mindfulness at Work

Several noteworthy cases shed light on the impact mindfulness can have on creativity and problem-solving in Silicon Valley. One such example is Twitter and Square co-founder, Jack Dorsey. An ardent champion of personal discipline and contemplative practice, Dorsey attributes a part of his balanced approach to entrepreneurship and solving complex problems to mindfulness.

General Mills, the corporation behind multinational technology company Bell Labs, also integrated a corporate mindfulness program, and what ensued was a significant increase in innovative thinking, improved ability to deal with stress, and heightened levels of focus among their employees. These are not isolated instances but part of an emerging and sustained trend of weaving mindfulness into the heart of the Valley's work culture.

8.4. The Neuroscientific Viewpoint

Considerable scientific evidence elucidates the impact of mindfulness on the functioning of the brain. It demonstrates that regular mindfulness practices can result in increased activities in brain regions associated with attention control, emotion regulation, and self-awareness, all of which support creative thinking and effective problem-solving.

This neuroscience research also shows that mindfulness meditation reduces activity in the default mode network (DMN), the brain network responsible for mind-wandering and self-referential thoughts. Reduced activity in the DMN can lead to less cognitive rigidity—an essential component for creative innovation and problem-solving.

8.5. A New Dawn for Problem Solving and Creativity

Mindfulness might seem like an esoteric addition to the tech world's ecosystem at first glance, but it is fast becoming a pillar of strength for creativity and problem-solving across Silicon Valley startups. As tech companies continue to foster the practice of mindfulness amongst their employees, one can't help but marvel at this harmonious blend of ancient wisdom and cutting-edge technology. This has planted mindfulness at the forefront of an exciting new surge in creative and effective problem-solving methods in the world's groundbreaking tech ecosystem.

Expanding on these fundamental ideas and case studies, we invite you to delve deeper into this riveting narrative of mindfulness in Silicon Valley. Witness how this amalgamation of 'mind tech' becomes the underlying modus operandi in the heartland of code and innovation. Unveiling the transformations one mindful moment at a time, this exploration becomes not just an observation but also a participation in this breathtaking evolution. Thus, Silicon Valley transforms into a beacon, illuminating the path towards mindful technological advancement.

Chapter 9. Case Studies: Success Stories and Lessons Learned

A decade ago, bringing up mindfulness in a corporate boardroom or a development pod would, at best, be met with dismissive chuckles. But as we approach the vortex of the 21st century's third decade, the fusion of ancient mindfulness practices and cutting-edge technology has moved from the fringy edges into the heart of Silicon Valley. Several startup success stories bear testimony to the benefits of incorporating mindfulness in the hectic worlds of code and design, venture capital, and software architecture. Let's delve deeper into these exciting experiences.

9.1. Dropbox: Mindfulness From the Top Down

Dropbox, the well-known file hosting service, provides an ideal example of a startup that has successfully integrated the culture of mindfulness. The company's co-founder, Drew Houston, is an ardent devotee of mindfulness, which he introduced into Dropbox's corporate culture. Under Houston's leadership, Dropbox implemented guided weekly meditations, silent mornings, and an open, well-lit meditation space in its San Francisco headquarters. These initiatives led to stark improvements in company synergy, employee productivity, and overall job satisfaction. By fostering mental awareness, Dropbox was not only able to reduce burnout rates among employees but also bolster its innovation and creativity, thereby driving a higher yield of successful projects.

9.2. Twitter and Square: Promoting Mental Fitness

Twitter and Square CEO Jack Dorsey, a vocal promoter of mindful practice, has made various efforts to incorporate meditation and mindfulness into both his personal life and his companies. Believing strongly in the power of mental fitness, Dorsey introduced weekly meditation classes at both Twitter and Square. His commitment to mindfulness reflects in his interactions with employees, approach to decision-making, and exercise of leadership influence. Dorsey's example thus demonstrates the possible impact when a leader lives by the principles of mindfulness and is committed to spreading its practice within an organization.

9.3. Google: "Search" Inside Yourself

A significant landmark in mindfulness implementation occurred when the tech giant Google introduced its "Search Inside Yourself" program. This initiative, started by early Google engineer Chade-Meng Tan, aimed to aid professionals in building emotional intelligence using mindfulness practices. The program's knock-on effects were extraordinary, resulting in improvements in leadership, productivity, creativity, stress management and, crucially, employee happiness. The success of "Search Inside Yourself" triggered a ripple effect across the Silicon Valley, inspiring countless other startups to adopt similar programs, which has significantly contributed to the valley's ongoing mindful revolution.

9.4. SAP: Mindfulness as a Productive Tool

Software company SAP offers another case study in successful implementation of mindfulness. Through their "Global Mindfulness

Practice" program, SAP's employees have the opportunity to participate in a wide variety of mindfulness sessions, which include 2-day mindfulness courses, and in-depth follow-up programs. The results? Increased productivity, improved focus, better decision-making capabilities, and a more content and harmonious workforce. SAP's Global Mindfulness Practice is now one of the largest corporate mindfulness programs worldwide.

9.5. Aetna: A Bottom-Line Impact

A dramatic example of mindfulness impact on a company's bottom line comes from health care benefits company Aetna. CEO Mark Bertolini introduced mindfulness-based programs into the company and encouraged employees to participate. Not only did this lead to a marked increase in employee engagement and satisfaction, but it also resulted in approximately $2000 per employee in healthcare costs savings and a $3000 per employee gain in productivity.

These real world case studies paint a clear picture of the positive impacts of mindfulness integration, both qualitatively and quantitatively. By nurturing mental health, improving focus, and fostering a better working environment, mindfulness leads to happier employees, faster innovation, and higher profits. While we have only touched the tip of the iceberg, the implications of mindfulness in workplaces promise to reshape the contours of corporate innovation and growth. And Silicon Valley, as always, remains at the forefront of this exciting revolution.

Chapter 10. The Challenges: Combating Skepticism and Maintaining Discipline

Though the practice of mindfulness has been embraced by numerous individuals in the tech industry, the journey to integrate this meditative discipline into Silicon Valley's vibrant startup scene hasn't been without its fair share of obstacles. With a culture steeped in data analytics and a worldview keenly focused on tangible and immediate results, the introduction of a philosophy grounded in age-old wisdom was sure to encounter resistance.

10.1. Skepticism: An Invisible Barrier

The valley was full of skeptics when the first attempts to implement mindful principles began. Many individuals, both executives and employees, questioned the potential benefits of mindfulness in a fast-paced, high-stress business environment. The practice, which for many seemed already shrouded in a general mysticism, appeared an inadequate answer to the peak levels of stress, crunch times, or the incessantly ticking product development counters.

Aside from personal doubts and the ingrained culture of disproving anything that doesn't stand solid in the face of metrics, the promotion of mindfulness was met with the Silicon Valley's signature brand of skepticism. There was a lack of hard, scientific proof that mindfulness could improve productivity, encourage a healthier work culture, or even reduce employee stress levels.

However, initiators had faith in the potential of mindfulness. Armed with anecdotal evidence and a small, yet growing body of research, they set about to challenge the lingering doubts. Promoting the philosophy became a mission, invigorated by their conviction that it could not only coexist with technological advancement but also augment its development effectively.

10.2. Struggle for Confirmation: The Role of Empirical Study

Efforts to generate quantifiable evidence regarding the benefits of mindfulness helped considerably in curbing skepticism. Early adopters collaborated with researchers from reputed institutions to scientifically measure the impact of mindfulness on individual employees and the workplace as a whole.

Numerous studies sprung up, focusing on aspects such as employee stress levels, decision-making abilities, productivity, work satisfaction, and even code quality. While results varied, an overall positive correlation began to surface, providing the hard data previously lacking and slowly eroding the throngs of skeptics.

10.3. Encouraging and Maintaining Discipline

One of the most significant challenges that emerged with the implementation of mindfulness in workplaces was maintaining the necessary discipline among participants. Getting people to attend initial mindfulness sessions was one hurdle; convincing them to incorporate daily mindfulness practices into their routine was another.

10.4. Boosting Participation and Regularity

To ensure employees felt motivated to participate, business leaders tailored the mindfulness program according to their specific corporate culture. They offered creative perks such as quiet rooms or dedicated time in the working schedule for employees to practice mindfulness. Providing training modules convenient for their workforce, regardless of their working shifts, also played a critical part in maintaining discipline.

One significant strategy used was linking mindfulness to individual betterment rather than forcing it as a company policy. This not only increased participation but also encouraged employees to include mindfulness practice in their personal routines outside the workplace.

10.5. Overcoming Challenges through Persistent Efforts

In the face of skepticism and struggles with discipline, advocates of mindfulness remained steadfast and continuously fine-tuned their approach to suit the unique context of a tech startup. They worked tirelessly to generate real-time data, develop appealing ways to engage employees, and create an environment conducive to mindful calculations amidst a whirlwind of data and code.

The journey of integrating mindfulness into the tech startup culture has indeed been challenging, but the resulting positive changes are a testament to the indomitable spirit of Silicon Valley. Not just a story of combatting skepticism and maintaining discipline, it's a narrative of how the mystic can coexist and harmonize the pragmatic, of how retrospection can enhance forward-thinking, and ultimately, how serenity can thrive amidst the unending storm of innovation.

The Silicon Valley's adoption of mindfulness has proven that technology and wisdom can indeed coexist and that the adoption of ancient lessons may well be the advanced answer for the future. The convergence of these two seemingly separated worlds engenders an evolution of the tech industry, one that's as promising as it promises to be perennial. Unfolding in the arena of crisp code and sharper algorithms, the story of this embrace is nothing short of revolutionary.

Chapter 11. The Future: Mindful Tech and Beyond

The transformation of Silicon Valley's startup scene into a cradle of mindful tech seems to be the product of a synergy of factors. The adoption of mindfulness practices in these companies is fuelled by a blend of ancient wisdom and cutting-edge techniques. This incorporation has been shown to not only foster a peaceful work environment but also stimulate efficiency and innovation.

11.1. Origins of Mindfulness in Tech

The origins of mindfulness in tech can be traced back to when stress and mental health issues started plaguing the startup industry. This pushed several founders, developers, and software engineers towards mindfulness as a potential solution to deal with burnout and stress.

The affinity of Silicon Valley's alpha-geeks towards Eastern wisdom was apparent. Heavyweights like Steve Jobs, who attributed a part of his creativity to Zen practice, had a profound influence on the undercurrents of Silicon Valley's culture.

11.2. The Present State of Mindful Tech

At present, there are several initiatives that incorporate mindfulness as a core principle within the tech industry. A testament to this is the proliferating number of tech companies offering mindfulness programs to their employees. Companies like Google and Salesforce have paved the ground by incorporating mindfulness teachings into their organizational culture, thereby inspiring scores of others across the industry.

Apple's 'Breathe' App on the Apple Watch and Google's 'Mindful Moments' represent attempts to embed mindfulness exercises directly into our routines. These applications serve as gentle reminders in a hectic world, nudging users to take a moment of resiliency.

11.3. The Role of Modern Innovation

Modern innovations have also played a dominant role in the emergence of mindful tech. Developments in neuro-feedback systems, for instance, that gauge brain signal patterns and provide real-time feedback, are aiding practitioners improve their mindfulness techniques.

Moreover, Virtual Reality (VR) has been capitalised on to provide immersive experiences such as tranquil forests or peaceful oceans, thereby facilitating mindfulness practices. This blend of digital technology with the ancient practice demonstrates how tech industries are innovating, providing mindfulness solutions.

11.4. Evidences of Efficacy

A plethora of studies reinforce the efficacy of mindfulness practices. Regular meditation reduces stress, improves cognition, and fosters empathy. When implemented in a work environment, these benefits translate into enhanced productivity, improved creativity, and a positive cultural ecosystem.

There's a myriad of evidence that startups incorporating mindfulness practices showed improved operational efficiencies, healthier work environments, and a significant reduction in employee burnout.

11.5. The Challenges

Integrating mindfulness into technology isn't smooth. Skepticism surrounds the concept of technologized mindfulness, questioning whether these practices might become shallow or lose their essence against the backdrop of commercial interests. Additionally, reports have emerged suggesting that excessive use of mindfulness apps, instead of inducing calmness, may trigger anxiety and dependency in some users.

11.6. Looking Ahead: The Future of Mindful Tech

The future will see more nuanced approaches to blending mindfulness and technology, devoid of over-reliance on gadgets. Hybrid strategies that take the best from both the old and the new—blending traditional approaches with the possibilities that technology allows, will become more popular.

As the tech industry grapples with the reality of mental health, we foresee a further surge in mindfulness programs. The arrival of newer technologies like 5G, AI and Machine Learning could pave the way for greater technological integration with mindfulness practices.

Mindful tech could very well become as ubiquitous as smartphones within the next few years. As mindfulness ascends from a 'nice to have' to a 'must have,' its integration into our work and personal life could become more seamless and necessary. This is not just another trend - it looks set to become the future of doing business.

Eventually, the goal wouldn't merely be about creating apps and gadgets that encourage mindful practices; rather, a holistic change, where every tech innovation is marked by a mindfulness-centric approach, could be the new norm. Indeed, as technology continues to shape and sometimes complicate our lives, it's comforting to envisage a future where it also assists us in reclaiming our peace and tranquillity. A paradox, yes, but a fascinating one, indeed.

The 'Buddha of Silicon Valley,' is well on its way, meandering through uncharted territories, sparking revolutions, and impacting humanity at a profound level.

9 798856 177076